The

QUOTABLE

LONGFELLOW

The

QUOTABLE

LONGFELLOW

Edited by MICHAEL STEERE

Introduction by Maine Poet Laureate
WESLEY McNAIR

Down East Books

CAMDEN, MAINE

Published by Down East Books
An imprint of Rowman & Littlefield
4501 Forbes Boulevard, Suite 200, Lanham, Maryland 20706
www.rowman.com

10 Thornbury Road, Plymouth PL6 7PP, United Kingdom

Distributed by National Book Network

British Library Cataloguing in Publication Information Available

Library of Congress Cataloging-in-Publication Data Available

ISBN 978-1-60893-261-0 (cloth : alk. paper)—ISBN 978-1-60893-262-7 (electronic)

∞™ The paper used in this publication meets the minimum requirements of
American National Standard for Information Sciences—Permanence of Paper
for Printed Library Materials, ANSI/NISO Z39.48-1992.

Printed in the United States of America

INTRODUCTION

During his lifetime Henry Wadsworth Longfellow was more popular in America than any poet has been before or since. His book-length narratives, such as *The Song of Hiawatha*, *Evangeline*, and *The Courtship of Miles Standish*, were reprinted dozens of times throughout the nineteenth century. *The Courtship of Miles Standish* sold twenty-five thousand copies in its first week of publication; in London, where Longfellow was also famous, ten thousand copies were sold in a single day. Americans everywhere learned his poems by heart, and children studied them in schools. On his seventieth birthday in 1877, there were public speeches, parades, and readings of his poetry at locations all over the nation.

His following diminished during the early-to-middle twentieth century. For the New Critics of that period, Longfellow, together with Tennyson and other poets of the 1800s, became the enemy. Guided by the precepts of John Crowe Ransom, they found his poetry sentimental, its emotion unchecked by irony. They also objected to Longfellow's tendency to draw meanings from his poems, which they called "moralizing." In the age of T. S. Eliot, whose poetry made its appeal to the intellect rather than to feeling, it was commonly assumed that a poem should contain its own meaning, to be revealed by the application of the mind. It did not seem to matter that Eliot published his central work, *The Waste Land*, with an array of footnotes to help readers interpret it.

But literary fashions change, and today it is not Longfellow but the New Critics who are under eclipse. American poets are no longer so suspicious of feeling; for some, in fact, it is a source of intelligence. The current aesthetic, together with historical perspective, have altered our view of Longfellow. Academics have written of his role in building the foundations of a national literature through his work, which included poetry, drama, fiction, nonfiction, anthologies, and translations. Cultural historians have credited Longfellow's popular epic poems with helping to forge an American identity in the early years of the nation's development. In 2003 the prestigious Library of America, dedicated to publishing authoritative editions of the nation's most significant writing, brought out an 854-page volume on Longfellow. And in the following year Charles Calhoun published a critically acclaimed biography of the poet, portentously titled *Longfellow: A Rediscovered Life*. These publications prepared the way for the bicentennial celebration of Longfellow's birthday in 2007, which featured the issuing of a stamp of the poet's likeness, together with a series of readings, concerts, and pageants throughout the country that rivaled the national birthday celebration of 1877.

As we consider Longfellow's resurgence, it's important to note that his readers never really forgot him; for they erected statues in his honor and named schools and parks after him for decades after his death. What inspired them was the emotional depth and music of his poetry. Though he may lack the originality of his contemporaries

Walt Whitman and Emily Dickinson, his power as a poet in such lyrics as "Snow-Flakes," "The Fire of Driftwood," "The Cross of Snow," "The Ropewalk," and "The Jewish Cemetery at Newport" remains undiminished.

The repossession of Henry Wadsworth Longfellow continues to the present, and this anthology of quotations is part of the ongoing appreciation of his work. Here, between covers for the first time, is wit and wisdom from Longfellow's lifetime as an author and observer. Some of the quotations come from his prose, and many others from his poetry, often from the same passages that the New Critics once dismissed for moralizing. A few of the metaphors Michael Steere has chosen—for instance, "Ships that pass in the night, and speak each other in passing," "footprints on the sands of time," and "Into each

life some rain must fall"—have become part of the common language.
There could be no surer proof of Longfellow's relevance and his
longevity.

WESLEY McNAIR
Maine Poet Laureate
Mercer, Maine

Most people would succeed in small things if they were not troubled with great ambitions.

Music is the universal language

of mankind.

A single conversation across the

table with a wise man is better than

ten years' mere study of books.

A torn jacket is soon mended;

but hard words bruise the heart

of a child.

All things come round to him

who will but wait.

Give what you have. To someone,

it may be better than you dare think.

He that respects himself is safe from others.

He wears a coat of mail that none can pierce.

What once has been shall be no more!

The groaning earth in travail and in pain

Brings forth its races, but does not restore,

And the dead nations never rise again.

If we could read the secret history

of our enemies we should find in

each man's life sorrow and suffering

enough to disarm all hostility.

I remember the gleams and glooms that dart

    Across the school-boy's brain;

The song and the silence in the heart,

    That in part are prophecies, and in part

Are longings wild and vain.

Perseverance is a great element of success. If you only knock long enough and loud enough at the gate, you are sure to wake up somebody.

It is foolish to pretend that one is

fully recovered from a disappointed

passion. Such wounds always

leave a scar.

Be still, sad heart! and cease repining;

Behind the clouds is the sun still shining;

Thy fate is the common fate of all;

Into each life some rain must fall.

We judge ourselves by what we feel

capable of doing, while others judge

us by what we have already done.

If you would hit the mark, you must

aim a little above it: Every arrow that

flies feels the pull of the earth.

And the night shall be filled with music,

And the cares, that infest the day,

Shall fold their tents like the Arabs,

and silently steal away.

Joy, temperance, and repose,

slam the door on the doctor's nose.

Love gives itself; it is not bought.

The heart, like the mind, has a memory.

And in it are kept the most precious keepsakes.

No endeavor is in vain;

Its reward is in the doing,

And the rapture of pursuing

Is the prize the vanquished gain.

The best thing one can do when it is

raining is to let it rain.

The mind of the scholar, if he would

leave it large and liberal, should

come in contact with other minds.

The nearer the dawn, the darker the night.

Whenever nature leaves a hole in a person's mind, she generally plasters it over with a thick coat of self-conceit.

That which the fountain sends forth

returns again to the fountain.

Simplicity in character, in manners, in style; in all things the supreme excellence is simplicity.

Ships that pass in the night, and speak each other in passing,

Only a signal shown, and a distant voice in the darkness;

So on the ocean of life, we pass and speak one another,

Only a look and a voice; then darkness again and a silence.

Not in the clamor of the crowded street,

Not in the shouts and plaudits of the throng,

But in ourselves, are triumph and defeat.

The talent of success is nothing more than doing what you can do well, and doing well whatever you do without thought of fame. If it comes at all it will come because it is deserved, not because it is sought after.

Then followed that beautiful season
. . . Summer . . . Filled was the air
with a dreamy and magical light; and
the landscape lay as if new created in
all the freshness of childhood.

A boy's will is the wind's will,

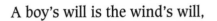

And the thoughts of youth are long, long thoughts.

A thought often makes us hotter

than a fire.

Ambition is so powerful a passion in the human breast, that however high we reach we are never satisfied.

One half of the world has to sweat

and groan, that the other half may

dream.

Build today, then strong and sure,

With a firm and ample base;

And ascending and secure.

Shall tomorrow find its place.

Critics are sentinels in the grand

army of letters, stationed at the

corners of newspapers and reviews,

to challenge every new author.

Every man has his secret sorrows

which the world knows not; and

often times we call a man cold

when he is only sad.

Evil is only good perverted.

With many readers the brilliance of

style passes for affluence of thought;

they mistake buttercups in the grass

for immeasurable gold mines under

ground.

Heights by great men reached and kept

Were not obtained by sudden flight

But they, while their companions slept,

They were toiling upward in the night.

However things may seem, no evil

thing is success and no good thing

is failure.

The life of a man consists not in

seeing visions and dreaming dreams,

but in active charity and willing

service.

In this world a man must either be

anvil or hammer.

Intelligence and courtesy not always are combined;

Often in a wooden house a golden room we find.

It is difficult to know at what moment love begins; it is less difficult to know that it has begun.

It takes less time to do a thing right, than it does to explain why you did it wrong.

Lives of great men all remind us,

We can make our lives sublime,

And, departing, leave behind us,

Footprints on the sands of time.

Look not mournfully into the past,

it comes not back again. Wisely

improve the present, it is thine. Go

forth to meet the shadowy future

without fear and with a manly heart.

Man is always more than he can

know of himself; consequently, his

accomplishments, time and again,

will come as a surprise to him.

Men of genius are often dull and

inert in society; as the blazing

meteor, when it descends to earth,

is only a stone.

People demand freedom only

when they have no power.

Sit in reverie and watch the changing color of the waves that break upon the idle seashore of the mind.

Within Earth's wide domains

    Are markets for men's lives;

Their necks are galled with chains,

    Their wrists are cramped with gyves. . . .

These are the woes of slaves;

    They glare from the abyss;

They cry, from unknown graves,

    "We are the Witnesses!"

If anybody wants to break a law,

let him break the Fugitive-Slave law.

That is all it is for.

Sometimes we may learn more from

a man's errors than from his virtues.

Talk not of wasted affection;

affection never was wasted.

The love of learning, the sequestered nooks,

And all the sweet serenity of books.

What would the world be to us

    If the children were no more?

We should dread the desert behind us

    Worse than the dark before.

They who go feel not the pain of

parting; it is they who stay behind

that suffer.

Whoever benefits his enemy with straightforward intention,

that man's enemies will soon fold their hands in devotion.

I do not believe anyone can be

perfectly well, who has a brain and

a heart.

Tell me not, in mournful numbers,

    Life is but an empty dream!

For the soul is dead that slumbers,

    And things are not what they seem.

Life is real! Life is earnest!

    And the grave is not its goal;

Dust thou art; to dust returnest,

    Was not spoken of the soul.

My soul is full of longing

For the secret of the sea,

And the heart of the great ocean

Sends a thrilling pulse through me.

Ah, how good it feels! The hand of

an old friend.

Thought takes man out of servitude,

into freedom.

The greatest firmness is the

greatest mercy.

For his heart was in his work, and

the heart giveth grace unto every art.

Each morning sees some task begun,

Each evening sees it close;

Something attempted, something done,

Has earned a night's repose.

"Wouldst thou."—so the helmsman answered,

"Learn the ways of the sea?

Only those who brave its dangers

Comprehend its mystery!"

. . . whither love aspires, there shall

my dwelling be.

Chill airs and wintry winds, my ear

    Has grown familiar with your song;

I hear it in the opening year,

    I listen, and it cheers me long.

O what a glory does this world put on

for him who, with a fervent heart, goes forth.

His brow is wet with honest sweat,

He earns whatever he can,

And looks the whole world in the face,

For he owes not any man.

I am in despair at the swift flight of

time, and the utter impossibility I feel

to lay upon anything permanent.

If thou art worn and hard beset

    With sorrows, that thou wouldst forget . . .

Go to the woods and hills, no tears

    Dim the sweet look that Nature wears.

The poverty-stricken millions

    Who challenge our wine and bread

And impeach us all as traitors,

    Both the living and the dead.

And whenever I sit at the banquet,

    Where the feast and song are high,

Amid the mirth and the music

    I can hear the fearful cry.

The every-day cares and duties,

which men call drudgery, are the

weights and counterpoises of the

clock of time.

Were half the power, that fills the world with terror,

Were half the wealth bestowed on camps and courts,

Given to redeem the human mind from error,

There were no need of arsenals or forts . . .

If you look about you, you will see men who are wearing life away in feverish anxiety of fame, and the last we shall ever hear of them will be the funeral bell.

In the mouths of many men soft

words are like roses that soldiers

put into the muzzles of their

muskets on holidays.

Beware of dreams! Beware of the

illusions of fancy! Beware of the

solemn deceivings of thy vast

desires!

Round about what is, lies a whole

mysterious world of might be—a

psychological romance of possibilities

and things that do not happen.

Every heart has its haunted chamber.

The Works of Henry Wadsworth Longfellow

Coplas de Don Jorge Manrique (translation from Spanish) (1833)

Outre-Mer: A Pilgrimage Beyond the Sea (travel essays) (1835)

Hyperion: A Romance (1839)

Voices of the Night (1839)

Ballads and Other Poems (1841)

Poems on Slavery (1842)

The Spanish Student: A Play in Three Acts (1843)

Poets and Poetry of Europe (translations) (1844)

The Belfry of Bruges and Other Poems (1845)

The Waif (anthology) (1845)

Evangeline: A Tale of Acadie (1847)

Kavanagh (1849)

The Seaside and the Fireside (1850)

The Golden Legend (1851)

The Song of Hiawatha (1855)

The Courtship of Miles Standish and Other Poems (1858)

The Children's Hour (1860)

Tales of a Wayside Inn (1863)

Birds of Passage (1863)

Household Poems (1865)

Flower-de-Luce (1867)

Dante's Divine Comedy (translation) (1867)

The New England Tragedies (1868)

The Divine Tragedy (1871)

Christus: A Mystery (1872)

Three Books of Song (1872)

Aftermath (1873)

Poems of Places (anthology) (1874)

The Masque of Pandora and Other Poems (1875)

Kéramos and Other Poems (1878)

Ultima Thule (1880)

In the Harbor (1882)

Michel Angelo: A Fragment (incomplete; published posthumously)